Popular Rock Superstars of Yesterday and Today

POP ROCK

AC/DC

Aerosmith

The Allman Brothers Band

The Beatles

Billy Joel

Bob Marley and the Wailers

Bruce Springsteen

The Doors

Elton John

The Grateful Dead

Led Zeppelin

Lynyrd Skynyrd

Pink Floyd

Queen

The Rolling Stones

U2

The Who

Queen

Peter Gregory

Mason Crest Publishers

Queen

Frontis True rock royalty, the rock band Queen made a long-lasting mark on the music world.

Produced by 21st Century Publishing and Communications, Inc.

Editorial by Harding House Publishing Services, Inc.

MASON CREST PUBLISHERS INC.
370 Reed Road
Broomall, Pennsylvania 19008
(866) MCP-BOOK (toll free)
www.masoncrest.com

Printed in the United States.

First Printing

9 8 7 6 5 4 3 2 1

Library of Congress Cataloging-in-Publication Data

Gregory, Peter, 1956–
    Queen / Peter Gregory.
       p. cm.—(Popular rock superstars of yesterday and today)
    Includes bibliographical references (p.   ) and index.
    Hardback edition: ISBN-13: 978-1-4222-0193-0
    Paperback edition: ISBN-13: 978-1-4222-0318-7
  1. Queen (Musical group)—Juvenile literature. 2. Rock musicians—England—
Biography—Juvenile literature. I. Title.
ML3930.Q44G74 2008
782.42166092'2—dc22
[B]   2007012146

Publisher's notes:
- All quotations in this book come from original sources, and contain the spelling and grammatical inconsistencies of the original text.

- The Web sites mentioned in this book were active at the time of publication. The publisher is not responsible for Web sites that have changed their addresses or discontinued operation since the date of publication. The publisher will review and update the Web site addresses each time the book is reprinted.

CONTENTS

1951
"Rocket 88," considered by many to be the first rock single, is released by Ike Turner.

1969
The Woodstock Music and Arts Festival attracts a huge crowd to rural upstate New York.

1952
DJ Alan Freed coins and popularizes the term "Rock and Roll," proclaimes himself the "Father of Rock and Roll," and declares, "Rock and Roll is a river of music that has absorbed many streams: rhythm and blues, jazz, rag time, cowboy songs, country songs, folk songs. All have contributed to the Big Beat."

1969
Tommy, the first rock opera, is released by British rock band The Who.

1970
The Beatles break up.

1967
The Monterey Pop Festival in California kicks off open air rock concerts.

1955
"Rock Around the Clock" by Bill Haley & His Comets is released; it tops the U.S. charts and becomes wildly popular in Britain, Australia, and Germany.

1971
Jim Morrison, lead singer of The Doors, dies in Paris.

1965
The psychedelic rock band, the Grateful Dead, is formed in San Francisco.

1971
Duane Allman, lead guitarist of the Allman Brothers Band, dies.

1950s

1960s

1970s

1957
Bill Haley tours Europe.

1969
A rock concert held at Altamont Speedway in California is marred by violence.

1974
Sheer Heart Attack by the British rock band Queen becomes an international success.

1957
Jerry Lee Lewis and Buddy Holly become the first rock musicians to tour Australia.

1969
The Rolling Stones tour America as "The Greatest Rock and Roll Band in the World."

1954
Elvis Presley releases the extremely popular single "That's All Right (Mama)."

1961
The first Grammy for Best Rock 'n' Roll Recording is awarded to Chubby Checker for *Let's Twist Again*.

1974
"Sweet Home Alabama" by Southern rock band Lynyrd Skynyrd is released and becomes an American anthem.

1964
The Beatles make their first visit to America, setting off the British Invasion.

1973
Rolling Stone magazine names Annie Leibovitz chief photographer and "rock 'n' roll photographer;" she follows and photographs rockers Mick Jagger, John Lennon, and others.

1987
Billy Joel becomes the first American rock star to perform in the Soviet Union since the construction of the Berlin Wall.

2005
Led Zeppelin is ranked #1 on VH1's list of the 100 Greatest Artists of Hard Rock.

1985
Rock stars perform at Live Aid, a benefit concert to raise money to fight Ethiopian famine.

2005
Many rock groups participate in Live 8, a series of concerts to raise awareness of extreme poverty in Africa.

2003
Led Zeppelin's "Stairway to Heaven" is inducted into the Grammy Hall of Fame.

1980
John Lennon of the Beatles is murdered in New York City.

1975
Tommy, the movie, is released.

2000s
Aerosmith's album sales reach 140 million worldwide and the group becomes the bestselling American hard rock band of all time.

2007
Billy Joel become the first person to sing the National Anthem before two Super Bowls.

1975
Time magazine features Bruce Springsteen on its cover as "Rock's New Sensation."

1995
The Rock and Roll Hall of Fame and Museum opens in Cleveland, Ohio.

1970s   1980s   1990s   2000s

1979
Pink Floyd's *The Wall* is released.

1991
Freddie Mercury, lead vocalist of the British rock group Queen, dies of AIDS.

2004
Elton John receives a Kennedy Center Honor.

1979
The first Grammy for Best Rock Vocal Performance by a Duo or Group is awarded to The Eagles.

2004
Rolling Stone Magazine ranks The Beatles #1 of the 100 Greatest Artists of All Time, and Bob Dylan #2.

1986
The Rolling Stones receive a Grammy Lifetime Achievement Award.

1981
MTV goes on the air.

2006
U2 wins five more Grammys, for a total of 22—the most of any rock artist or group.

1986
The first Rock and Roll Hall of Fame induction ceremony is held; Chuck Berry, Little Richard, Ray Charles, Elvis Presley, and James Brown, are among the first inductees.

1981
For Those About to Rock We Salute You by Australian rock band AC/DC becomes the first hard rock album to reach #1 in the U.S.

2006
Bob Dylan, at age 65, releases *Modern Times* which immediately rises to #1 in the U.S.

Years of hard work paid off when Queen received VH1 Rock Honors in 2006. There to accept the award were (left to right) vocalist Paul Rodgers, guitarist Brian May, and drummer Roger Taylor. Two of the original members couldn't attend: Freddie Mercury, who died several years before, and John Deacon.

Queen Is Crowned

May 25, 2006, was a big night at the Mandalay Bay Event Center in Las Vegas, Nevada. Metal music was getting its "props" when the popular resort hosted the VH1 Rock Honors. Members of the music world came together to celebrate the groundbreaking influence of four of metal music's biggest names: Queen, Kiss, Def Leppard, and Judas Priest.

A Night to Remember

For those gathered at the Mandalay Bay Event Center that evening, it would a night they would remember for a long time. According to VH1,

> **"Each year, the Rock Honors show shines the spotlight to explain the honorees' unique sound, and measuring the influence each has had on a particular genre of modern music."**

The groups honored that evening certainly met those qualifications. Those showing their appreciation of the groups' music extended beyond the "usual suspects" of the recording industry. Among those paying their respects were actors Kiefer Sutherland, Gina Gershon, Jamie Kennedy, Natasha Henstridge, and Brittany Snow, as well as magician Penn Jillette.

But the stars of the evening were the musicians, and the evening opened with a bang. Queen's Brian May and Roger Taylor took the stage with the Foo Fighters for a rocking performance of Queen's "Tie Your Mother Down." Paul Rodgers joined Queen to perform a **medley** of the group's best-known songs. "We Will Rock You," and "We Are the Champions" were sung from the stage, as well as from the audience. It was clear that even after many years, those songs remained in the memories of many.

Although not generally known as a metal band, Queen did influence many in that genre. Those truly knowledgeable of the music scene have acknowledged Queen's influence on contemporary rock music for quite some time. In fact, the VH1 Rock Honors was not the first time it had been singled out for the group's uniqueness and importance to the history of rock music.

The Hall Calls

Ten years after the death of Freddie Mercury, Queen's energetic lead singer and pianist, the group was **inducted** into the Rock and Roll Hall of Fame. Like those elected to other halls of fame, such as sports, inductees into the Rock and Roll Hall of Fame must have made special contributions to their fields and meet specific guidelines before they can even be considered for membership in the hall.

The road to the Rock and Roll Hall of Fame is not an easy one, even for those who meet the **criteria**. Performers become eligible for consideration twenty-five years after the release of their first recording. A nominating committee consisting of rock 'n' roll historians evaluates each performer eligible for nomination on their influence on and importance to rock music. After careful deliberations, the nominating committee decides who will be on the ballot. The ballots are sent to more than 1,000 rock music experts, who then vote on who will make it into the Rock and Roll Hall of Fame. Those with the highest number of votes, and who have more than 50 percent of the vote, are elected into the hall. On average, only five to seven performers are inducted into the hall each year.

Queen's Turn

On March 19, 2001, it was Queen's turn to accept the hall's invitation. The ballroom of the luxurious Waldorf-Astoria Hotel in New York City was filled with rock legends for the 16th Annual Rock and Roll Induction Ceremony. Other members of the Class of 2001 included Aerosmith, Solomon Burke, the Flamingos, Michael Jackson, Paul Simon, Steely Dan, and Ritchie Valens.

Queen's role in rock history was cemented with its induction into the Rock and Roll Hall of Fame in March 2001. Ceremony attendees were treated to a rockin' performance of "We Will Rock You" and "Tie Your Mother Down" by Brian May (seen in this photo) and Roger Taylor, along with Foo Fighters Dave Grohl and Taylor Hawkins.

The 2000s brought award after award to Queen. In 2002, Brian and Roger accepted on star on the Hollywood Walk of Fame on behalf of the rock group. Queen became the first group inducted into the Songwriters Hall of Fame in 2003, and in 2004, the group was inducted into the UK Music Hall of Fame.

Dave Grohl and Taylor Hawkins of the Foo Fighters presented Queen for induction. Guitarist Brian May and drummer Roger Taylor were there to accept the honor. John Deacon was scheduled to attend but was forced to cancel. Sadly, the ceremony came ten years after the death of Freddie Mercury, who died in 1991 of complications of AIDS. His mother, Jer Bulsara, accepted the honor on behalf of Freddie.

Queen played its megahit "We Will Rock You." Dave joined the group and sang lead on "Tie Your Mother Down." He was as excited as any Queen fan would have been that night:

> **"John Deacon didn't come out tonight, but even two members of Queen is more than you'd ever imagine being on stage with. I mean, dude, it's Queen."**

When a member asked Dave if the Foo Fighters had decided what song Queen would perform, he replied, "We didn't pick the song, it's Queen!"

The British Hall

The United States was not the only country to recognize Queen's importance to rock history. In 2004, the United Kingdom inducted the first members into its Music Hall of Fame, and Queen was a part of the initial class.

Selection into the hall is handled a bit differently in the United Kingdom. Awards are divided into Honorary and Popular. A panel selects those who receive honorary membership in the hall. In 2004, Madonna, Bob Marley, U2, Elvis Presley, and the Beatles were selected for honorary membership.

Viewers of a BBC television show selected popular honorees, with a musical act chosen to represent each decade, beginning with the 1950s. They chose Queen to represent the 1970s, and Justin Hawkins of the Darkness presented Queen's award. Others who were selected for popular membership were Cliff Richard (1950s), the Rolling Stones (1960s), Michael Jackson (1980s), and Robbie Williams (1990s).

Queen has known success for more than thirty years. And to think it all began with a Smile.

When Freddie Mercury, Brian May, Roger Taylor, and John Deacon first got together in the early 1970s in Britain, little could they have imagined the heights their new group—Queen—would reach. They would become world famous and play an important role in rock 'n' roll history. But it wasn't always an easy road.

2

A Regal Vision

Throughout history, teens have loved music. Brian May, Roger Taylor, John Deacon, and Freddie Bulsara were no exceptions. They loved music, and they played every chance they could, even if that meant changing bands to do so. Their experiences with other bands would eventually bring them together to form Queen.

Introducing . . .

Brian played guitar, Roger played drums, and Tim Staffell played bass for Smile, a band that played around London. Freddie Bulsara was one of Tim's closest friends. Tim introduced Freddie to Brian and Roger and invited him to rehearsals. After Tim left Smile, Freddie joined Roger and Brian to keep the group going.

Freddie didn't like the name Smile, and he convinced the others to change the group's name to Queen. According to Freddie:

> **"The concept of Queen is to be regal and magestic. Glamour is part of us and we want to be dandy."**

Freddie also decided to change his own last name, and Freddie Bulsara became Freddie Mercury.

Something Different

In 1971, John Deacon joined Queen as the bass player. The group worked hard, fine-tuning their sound. During the early 1970s, glam rock (sometimes called glitter rock) was big in England. T. Rex's Marc Bolan is often credited as the creator of glam rock. Other glam rockers included the early Elton John, David Bowie in his Ziggy Stardust phase, Gary Glitter, and Alice Cooper. Musicians often dressed in ways that made it unclear whether they were male or female. Showmanship was the rule. The cult classic film *The Rocky Horror Picture Show* gives a good idea of what glam rock was all about.

Hard Rock, Queen's Way

Hard rock was also popular in the early 1970s. Definitions of hard rock are as varied as the groups who played it. It is often confused with heavy metal, and there is crossover. Some music historians say the difference between the two is more image than music.

Hard rock features electric guitars (often with their sound distorted), bass guitar, and drums. There is also a strong influence of the **blues**, especially a style known as British Blues with its use of keyboards and an electronic bass. Groups such as AC/DC and Aerosmith are among the best-known hard-rock musicians.

These music forms were among the most popular in Britain as Queen developed its unique sound. In June 1971, the group played its first public concert. Finally, in 1973, Queen was ready for their record debut. The guys were on their way.

Despite positive responses from critics, Queen's first album, *Queen*, wasn't a big seller. *Queen II*, released the following year, reached #5 on the album charts. Freddie Mercury—songwriter—had his first hit with the single "Seven Seas of Rhye," which cracked the top-10 charts. While waiting for their first international hit, Queen toured with Mott the Hoople in 1973.

Queen helped spread the hard-rock style of rock 'n' roll across the United Kingdom and the United States. With John on bass, Brian on guitar, and Roger on drums, Queen's pulsating rhythms touched the audience from head to toes. When Freddie's vocals and keyboard antics were added, Queen became unique.

Not *That* Queen

Queen toured Australia in 1974, but it was a complete disaster. Brian developed an illness from his pre-trip shots. Australian roadies resented the fact the group brought its own lights and crew. Equipment was sabotaged. Freddie got an ear infection. The crowd wanted to hear Australian bands, not something called Queen. Even the paparazzi weren't happy. More than once the press showed up at Queen appearances expecting the Queen of England. Imagine their surprise when the guys appeared!

International success came with the release in 1974 of *Sheer Heart Attack*. For the first time, Queen found success in the United States; the album went **gold**. The album included ballads, heavy metal, and ragtime- and Caribbean-influenced songs. A single from the album, "Killer Queen," was a hit in Britain and the United States.

In this photo, John, Freddie, Brian, and Roger pose for the cover of their 1974 album *Sheer Heart Attack*. The album took Queen to the big time—success in the United States. The album went gold, and the group became an international success. Never again would this Queen of England be confused with the other Queen!

Finding Their Way

In 1975, Queen had its first true megahit with *A Night at the Opera*. The title came from a 1935 Marx Brothers' movie with same name. Fans and critics loved the album. It reached #1 in Britain and #4 on the U.S. album charts, where it eventually went three times **platinum**. Sales are always important, but for this one, it was even more important that fans bought the album: at the time, *A Night at the Opera* was the most expensive album ever produced.

The album spun off one of Queen's most important and biggest-selling singles, "Bohemian Rhapsody." It was also their first song with a video. In Britain, it stayed on the top of the charts for nine weeks. At seven minutes, it was too long to get much airplay in the United States, where most records were no more than two or three minutes. Since airplay was important to record sales, an edited version of the song was released in the United States. It worked. The song played extensively on U.S. radio stations, and it hit #9 on the singles chart.

Another hit from the album was "You're My Best Friend." It didn't chart quite as high as "Bohemian Rhapsody" in the United States, reaching only #16, but worldwide it cracked almost all top-10 lists.

In 1975, Queen embarked on their first U.S. tour. Several dates had to be canceled, however, when Freddie developed throat problems. After a brief rest, the sellout tour continued.

Queen also toured Japan in 1975, where crowds of thousands met the group. The guys couldn't go anywhere without a group of screaming fans following them; it was total Queenmania. Though they might not have known what the words meant, fans knew what they were and sang along with the group during their concerts.

The following year, the group released *A Day at the Races*. Again the group borrowed a title from a Marx Brothers' movie, this one from 1937. Despite being popular with fans and critics, it didn't have the same success as *A Night at the Opera*.

The breakout single from the album, "Somebody to Love," reached #13 in the United States and #2 in Britain. The main influence for the song was **gospel** music. Freddie, Brian, and Roger recorded their voices multiple times to create the sound of a gospel choir of more than one hundred!

A Whirlwind in 1976

Queen began 1976 with a U.S. tour. Though "Bohemian Rhapsody" and *A Night at the Opera* had been doing well, sales and airplay soared after the group toured. After its successful U.S. tour, Queen returned to Japan, and then went back to Australia. The guys were uncertain about returning to Australia. After all, their 1974 visit was less than memorable—at least in a good way. This time, though, it was completely different. Each concert was sold out, and there was no question among paparazzi of which Queen would show up!

In 1976, Queen performed at one of its best-known concerts. The free concert, held at London's Hyde Park in September, commemorated the anniversary of Jimi Hendrix's death. Kiki Dee and Supercharge were among the other performers. Officially, 150,000 people attended, but estimates place the actual number at between 180,000 and 200,000.

The concert was a huge success and meant a lot to Queen. On the Web site www.Queenzone.com, Brian is quoted:

> **"I think that Hyde Park was one of the most significant gigs in our career. There was a great affection because we'd kind of made it in a lot of countries by that time, but England was still, you know, we weren't really sure if we were really acceptable here. So it was a wonderful feeling to come back and see that crowd and get that response."**

Apparently, even rock stars can be insecure!

Back to the Studio

As much as Queen loved to tour, the guys knew they had to cut another album. Fans liked the 1977 album, *News of the World*; it would eventually be certified multi-platinum. But most critics hated it. It would take years before it would be recognized as one of the best hard-rock albums of the late 1970s.

Two of the group's biggest singles came from that album. People either hate or love "We Will Rock You" and "We Are the Champions"; there seems to be no middle ground when it comes to these songs. Both reached #4 on U.S. charts. Perhaps more important, these songs

The United States had Beatlemania during the 1960s, and in 1975, Japan experienced Queenmania. The Japanese couldn't get enough of Queen. The guys were trailed by screaming fans, clamoring to get something that belonged to the beloved group. Freddie loved performing in Japan. He loved the people and the culture. He became a respected collector of Japanese art.

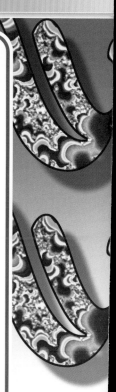

have become vital parts of the U.S. sports scene. In sports **venues** across the country, they are as much a part of sport as singing "Take Me Out to the Ballgame" during baseball's seventh-inning stretch. In many cases, the songs—or parts of them—are sung **a cappella**. And sung might be a stretch to describe the crowd performance, especially of "We Will Rock You." The non-musically inclined can feel comfortable chanting the words, followed naturally by hand-clapping and foot-stomping at the end of "We will, we will rock you."

For the first time, Queen seemed to disappoint their fans with their next album, *Jazz*, in 1978. It wasn't a hit with the critics either. Queen fans bought the album, though in fewer numbers than in the past. It reached platinum status, and for many groups that would be great. But this was Queen, and the band was used to its albums becoming *multi*-platinum.

Ending the Decade

The guys were disappointed and decided to regroup. Slowing down seemed like a good idea. Except for a live album released in 1979, they spent the rest of the decade working on one album. That album would bring them their first #1 single in the United States.

Queen's 1979 album, *Live Killers*, ended the decade on an up note for the group and returned Queen to its multi-platinum sales status. The band began the 1980s with high hopes for continued success.

The decade began with fans enthusiastically waiting for the latest Queen album. Queen's fans were loyal, and *Jazz* hadn't dampened their love for the group. They'd proven that by making *Live Killers* multi-platinum. And when *The Game* was released in 1980, it became the group's highest-selling, non–greatest-hits album of all time. It also reached #1 on the U.S. album charts; *The Game* went multi-platinum.

The Game also spun off two singles that were astronomical sellers. The **rockabilly** song "Crazy Little Thing Called Love" became Queen's first #1 single in the United States in February 1981; it was certified gold. Fans were crazy about the song. It was impossible to sit still while listening to its bouncy rhythms and Freddie's voice.

"Another One Bites the Dust"

The Game's "Another One Bites the Dust" was released as a single during the summer of 1980. The song wasn't intended to be a single,

As much as groups might love to tour, they have to spend time in the not-so-glamorous recording studio as well. After the wildly successful Japan tour, Queen returned to the recording studio to produce its next album. In this photo, Freddie and John work on *News of the World*, which was released in 1977.

When Queen played a stadium, they *filled* the stadium. More than once, Queen broke concert attendance records, including performances in South America and Mexico. Fans came from hundreds of miles just to experience the excitement—and killer music—at a Queen concert. And it would be an experience few of them would ever forget.

but Freddie's friend, pop star Michael Jackson, convinced them it would be a big hit. His instinct proved to be right. In October, the song hit the top of the U.S. singles chart, and it reached multi-platinum status, selling more than seven million copies. It became the first song to place on the *Billboard* Rock, R&B, and Dance charts at the same time. Queen's only Grammy nomination was for "Another One Bites the Dust." However, Bob Seger won for "Against the Wind."

Not all was rosy for Queen in 1980. The group's soundtrack for the film *Flash Gordon* also came out in 1980, but its sales were poor. It did reach the top-10 in Britain, though.

A Year of Firsts: 1981

It would be hard for Queen to beat the success they experienced in 1980. Though 1981 wasn't as successful as the previous year, for Queen it was the opportunity to do two new things: tour South America and collaborate with another artist.

Rock bands had toured South America before but not *big* stars. Queen was the first. In 1981, the group became the first major rock band to play every major stadium in South America. In São Paulo, Brazil, more than 250,000 people attended Queen concerts over two days, the largest paying audience to hear one band. Queen played before a total of 479,000 fans during their South American tour.

Brian found the tour reinvigorating:

"It's a long time since we've experienced such warmth from a new audience. We feel really good about it now, as our ambitions have been partly realised."

After South America, Queen played three concerts in Mexico. As in South America, Queen was the first major rock band to play concerts in that country. More than 150,000 Mexican fans were treated to live Queen concerts.

Queen returned to the studio after their highly successful tour. One day David Bowie dropped by. He and the guys jammed for a while, and worked on a song. "Under Pressure" resulted. Queen was happy with it, but David apparently wasn't so pleased; he didn't play it for several years. Fans liked it; it reached #1 in Britain and #29 on the U.S. *Billboard* singles charts.

In 1981, Queen's first greatest-hits album was released, featuring the group's work between 1974 and 1980. There was no doubt that the group had found success.

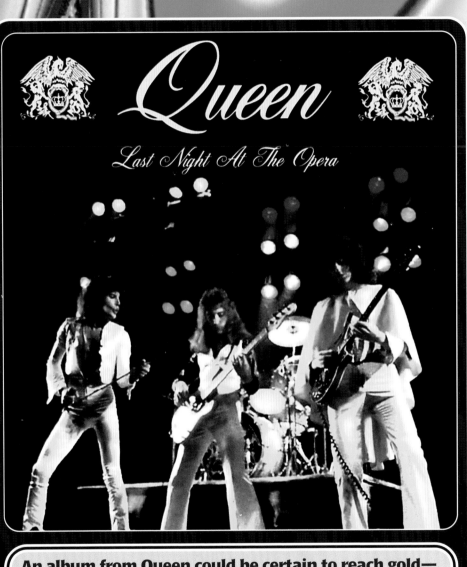

Queen

Last Night At The Opera

An album from Queen could be certain to reach gold—at the least. Fans worldwide could listen to and enjoy the group's music on an album. But no matter how good an album's technical quality was, it was not the same thing as seeing the guys perform in person, especially as part of a very large group of Queen fans.

3

Appearing Live

Musicians have to pay their dues before they find success. Queen knew that, but the band members had a long-term vision of how they wanted their career to develop—and it didn't include playing gigs at clubs and bars around London. Instead, they worked to develop a *show*, an experience that would be remembered long after it was over.

Freddie could put on a show; there was no arguing with that. He was in complete command when onstage. Even when he had played years earlier with a band called Ibex, during his pre-Queen days, he was sowing the seeds of the performer whose onstage antics would become almost legendary. Ken Testi, who had been a manager and roadie with Ibex, said of Freddie,

Freddie was unique. He captured every member of the audience with the first note that left his mouth, and held them until he sang the last note of the performance. It was a talent that few other frontmen then or now can claim. But it was one they all wished they had.

"He took it over the edge. And of course, I always admired a man who wears tights. I only saw him in concert once, and as they say, he was definitely a man who could hold an audience in the palm of his hand.**"**

A Queen concert was huge, and not just in its importance or the excitement it caused. Physically, a Queen show was huge. The size of their shows, including that of equipment such as the lighting rig, meant that a Queen concert could not fit just anywhere. Stadiums and arenas were necessary for a Queen concert, but they had lots of seats. If many of those seats remained empty, well, that could be embarrassing to the group. That wasn't a problem for Queen. The band played in large-audience venues, and seldom was an empty seat to be found. Its first public performance had been before a small, invited audience. Now, Queen concerts were often sold out shortly after tickets went on sale, and the group was responsible for breaking attendance records.

Taking a Break

In 1982, Queen was back in the recording studio, again looking for a unique sound. Yes, the group was different from many other rock groups, but it was also interested in doing something different from what it had done before, pushing the envelope on what the guys could do and how the audience would perceive them. Brian, Roger, John, and Freddie tried to take a slight detour from the tried and true when it came to their next album. "Another One Bites the Dust" had been a huge hit for them a few years before, and the guys thought they could build on that success with an album that contained more dance and **funk** music. For this album, Queen would set aside its hard-rock roots. But the result of the latest experiment, *Hot Space*, was a big disappointment to many of Queen's fans. Over the years, the fans had come to expect a certain level of quality from the guys. Many felt Queen didn't deliver in this 1982 release.

Queen also toured North America for the last time in 1982. Record sales had been slipping in the United States, and touring was expensive, especially for a show as big as the one Queen put on for its audiences. In the end, it all boiled down to business, and the guys made the tough decision that it really wasn't a smart business move to continue touring there. On September 15, 1982, Queen played at the Great Western Forum in Inglewood, California. That was the last time Freddie Mercury and Queen performed in the United States.

Few bands worked harder than Queen had for ten years. Many people, including the guys in the band, felt as though they had either been touring or recording constantly during that decade. As 1982 came to a close, the members decided they needed a break from such a grueling schedule—and from each other. Most of the guys had solo projects that interested them, and this vacation gave them the opportunity to pursue their individual interests. As often happens with music groups, this time away from performing as a group led to rumors that Queen was breaking up. Had slipping record sales in the United States, an important market, led to **dissension** within the band? Were Freddie's antics becoming too much for the other guys? Though the rumors would persist for the rest of the group's career, there's no real evidence that the band was ever close to splitting.

Going Solo

This wasn't the first time members of Queen had ventured out on their own. In 1977, Roger had released his first single, "I Wanna Testify." Freddie had performed with the Royal Ballet in London in 1979. The orchestra played while Freddie sang live and "danced"; his performance brought the audience to their feet in thunderous applause. Roger's second single and a solo album were released in 1981.

Now during this break, Roger worked on a project with Eddie Van Halen of the rock group Van Halen. *Star Fleet Project* was released in 1983. Freddie also worked on non-Queen projects. In 1983, he began work on a solo album, but he was interrupted when the world of film called his name. (His solo album, *Mr. Bad Guy*, wouldn't be completed and released for another two years.) A re-release of the classic 1926 silent film *Metropolis* was in the works, and Georgio Moroder, who spearheaded the project, wanted contemporary music for the film. He asked Freddie to write a song for the film, and "Love Kills" became part of *Metropolis*.

Opera also caught Freddie's attention during the vacation from Queen. In 1983, he saw a performance of the opera *Un Ballo in Maschera*. Performing was Montserrat Caballé, and her voice inspired

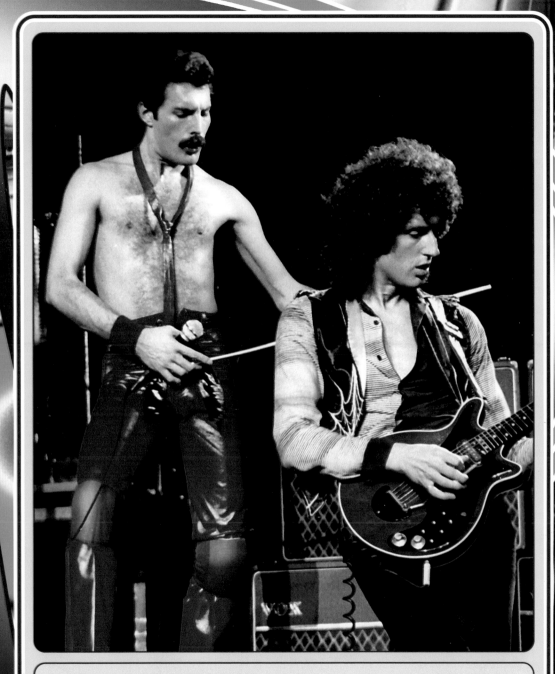

In 1982, Freddie (left), Brian (right), and the rest of the band decided to cut back on their tour schedule. The guys also decided to cut back on recording as well. Though they liked each other, the past several years had brought almost constant togetherness. They needed to take a break.

Freddie to write for her. Another four years went by, however, before he was able to work with her on a project.

The time apart was never meant to be permanent. In fact, Queen did get together during 1983 to work on its next album, *The Works*, which was released in 1984. The album spawned four hit singles:

A break from Queen did not mean that the guys spent the entire time vacationing and relaxing. Most had projects that interested them, but the intense schedule as part of Queen wouldn't let the guys follow through on those interests. For example, Roger now had time to work with Eddie Van Halen on *Star Fleet Project*.

"Radio Ga Ga," "I Want to Break Free," "Hammer to Fall," and "Tear It Up." "Radio Ga Ga" was the group's last top-40 hit in the United States until 1992. The album didn't sell especially well in the United States, reaching only #16.

South Africa

Controversy also reached Queen in 1984 when the group returned to touring with a concert series in South Africa. At the time, the country of South Africa had a strict policy of apartheid. People in the African nation were separated on the basis of their color. Most governments and people of the Western world rejected apartheid. The outcry of governments, people, and business increased as news of what was going on in South Africa, including the imprisonment of Nelson Mandela in 1964, became known. Many governments placed restrictions and prohibitions on doing business with South Africa. Even where restrictions did not exist, people often boycotted anything to do with South Africa. Even South African athletes felt the backlash of their country's policy; South Africa was banned from competing at the Olympics from 1964 until 1992.

It was against this political background that Queen went to South Africa. It wasn't the first time their tour schedule had invited controversy; not everyone had been pleased with the group's trip to South America, since many Western governments were opposed to the policies of some South America countries. However, by comparison, that tour resulted in little controversy. When Queen returned from performing in the segregated country in South Africa, a storm of criticism met the group. The guys responded by telling critics that they had played for the people, not the government; besides, audiences for their performances had been integrated. Queen's music was for everyone.

After some much needed time apart, Brian, Freddie, John and Roger (seen left to right in this photo) came back together and picked up where they left off. Though record sales were sluggish at first, crowds still came by the thousands to be a part of a Queen concert. Queen was still extremely popular.

The Best and the Worst

Slipping record sales could have signaled the end of Queen's high ride in popularity. But the group needn't have worried. Though few might have thought it possible, Queen broke its own concert attendance record in 1985. Queen opened and closed the Rock in Rio festival, playing before a sold-out crowd of 250,000 both nights. But that was just the beginning.

In July, musicians were coming together in London and Philadelphia for Live Aid, a concert designed to bring attention to starvation in Ethiopia. In 1984, rocker Bob Geldof of the Boomtown Rats had put together a group of British and Irish musicians, which he called Band Aid. Among the participants were some of the biggest names in music: Bono, Phil Collins, Sting, David Bowie, Paul McCartney, and Boy George. The group recorded "Do They Know It's Christmas." Proceeds from the sale of the single went to help the ease famine in Ethiopia. Bob Geldof hoped to build on the success of the record with something much bigger and much more elaborate, something perfectly suited for Queen.

Live Aid

It sounded like the perfect venue for Queen—Wembley Stadium in London. Musicians would also gather at JFK Stadium in Philadelphia for the concert that would be broadcast to more than 100 countries. Cutting-edge technology would be instrumental to the fund-raiser's success. But despite the apparently good fit between the band and Live Aid, the band said no when asked. What it hadn't counted on was Bob Geldof's stubbornness to get what he wanted—and he wanted Queen. He contacted the group, then contacted the group again and again, until he finally wore the guys down and they agreed to be part of the concert. Queen performed some of its best-known and most successful songs. More than 1.5 billion people, live and in television audience, had the opportunity to witness the showmanship that had set the group apart from others almost since the beginning. To most, Queen stole the show, and that's saying a lot, since other performers included U2, Mick Jagger, Tina Turner, and David Bowie.

Live Aid did something for Queen as well. Sales of the group's recordings increased, and it had a new vitality. Queen ended 1985 with "One Vision," a song that was featured in the film *Iron Eagle*. The band was always looking for new venues for their music, including film. Freddie said,

"I hate doing the same thing again and again. I like to see what's happening now in music, film and theatre and incorporate all of those things."

The Close of a Decade

The rest of the 1980s were busy for the members of Queen. In 1986, Queen recorded *A Kind of Magic*. The Magic Tour stop at Wembley Stadium was recorded and released as a double album. To many, that album is the ultimate Queen live album. More than 125,000 attended the stop at Knebworth Park, the group's 685th concert. Little did they know at the time, but they had just seen the group's last performance.

For Freddie, his first solo album, *Mr. Bad Guy* (dedicated to his cats) was released in 1985. His long-awaited project with opera star Montserrat Caballé, *Barcelona*, finally came out in 1988. He also worked on some musical projects with Michael Jackson, though none have been formally released.

After releasing its album *The Miracle* in 1989, Queen announced it would not go on tour to support the album. This was almost unheard of, especially for Queen; this was a band who seemed to live to tour. Again rumors flew that the group was breaking up. This time, though, another rumor was making the rounds, and this one *was* true. Freddie Mercury was seriously ill.

In 1985, a group of concerned musicians joined together to raise awareness and donations to combat famine in Africa, especially in Ethiopia. From a collection of music legends, Queen stood apart, bringing down the house during its performance at London's Wembley Stadium. Here, Freddie and others come together for the concert finale.

Loss of an Icon

Freddie's really sick. Freddie's dying. No, Freddie's just tired. Freddie's well-being had been the subject of speculation since the early 1980s. He denied all the rumors, but it was obvious to anyone who followed Queen that something was seriously wrong with the powerhouse. Still, he and Queen pressed on, releasing "Innuendo" in 1991.

The single became #1 in the United Kingdom, and when the album was released later, it took over the top spot on the album charts. The album *Innuendo* reached #30 in the United States. The renewed interest spurred their record company to re-release the group's entire catalogue. The tracks were re-mastered, and many of the newer versions include songs that did not appear on the original albums.

There had been no tour for *The Miracle*, and the guys announced that they would not tour for *Innuendo* either, fanning the flames of the rumor that Freddie's health was worsening. Instead of a tour, Brian appeared at radio stations around the United Kingdom, plugging the album and its singles, as well as his own solo album, which was due for release later that year. In October, Queen released its second greatest-hits album.

Freddie was seen in public less and less often. When he was, such as at an awards ceremony in 1990 to achieve a lifetime achievement award, he wore heavy layers of makeup. This managed to fool few; instead, it only increased talk that Freddie was ill. Finally, Freddie decided to let his many friends and fans know the truth. On November 23, 1991, he released the following statement:

> **"Following the enormous conjecture in the press over the last two weeks, I wish to confirm that I have been tested HIV positive and have AIDS. I felt it correct to keep this information private to date to protect the privacy of those around me. However, the time has come now for my friends and fans around the world to know the truth, and I hope that everyone will join with my doctors and all those worldwide in the fight against this terrible disease. My privacy has always been very special to me, and I am famous for my lack of interviews. Please understand this policy will continue."**

DAILY STAR

BRITAIN'S BRIGHTEST NEWSPAPER

Only 25p ...

FREDDIE MERCURY: LAST TRAGIC HOURS

AIDS KILLS THE KING OF ROCK

Queen's world, and that of rock music as a whole, received a tragic blow in 1991, when Freddie died from complications of AIDS. Freddie's death was cover news for many newspapers, including London's *Daily Star*. Rumors about his health had persisted for years, but it was still difficult to believe that Freddie Mercury, who had once seemed unstoppable, was gone.

The music world was in shock. It was one thing to suspect that something was wrong, but now there was no question about it. Plus, the news was worse than what many had expected. In the early 1990s, people diagnosed with AIDS generally didn't live very long. Drug cocktails, which now allow people living with AIDS to maintain a high quality of life for many years, were in their infancy in the early 1990s.

The world had little time to process what Freddie had admitted. The next day, forty-five-year-old Freddie Mercury, who had once seemed to have the going power of the Energizer Bunny, died at his home.

On his death, Brian, John, and Roger released the following statement:

> **"We have lost the greatest and most beloved member of our family. We feel overwhelming grief that he has gone, sadness that he should be cut down at the height of his creativity, but above all great pride in the courageous way he lived and died. It has been a privilege for us to have shared such magical times. As soon as we are able, we would like to celebrate his life in the style to which he was accustomed."**

Freddie would have liked that.

Saying Good-Bye

Fans felt as though a good friend had been snatched from them, and many needed to let others know how they felt. Flowers and messages from all over the world were sent to Queen's offices. A double layer of flowers covered the large lawn at Freddie's home. Fans stood waiting outside the gates of Freddie's home. No one seemed to know what they were waiting for; they just needed to be there, near something that had belonged to Freddie. Some stood for hours, and many had tear-stained faces. The night before the funeral, his family opened the gates to his home so his fans could come in, see the flowers, and leave their own messages of sympathy for Freddie's family and the other members of Queen.

Freddie's funeral was conducted in Zoroastrian tradition, his family's faith, although he had stopped practicing many years before.

His body was cremated, and there has been much speculation about what became of his ashes. Some people think they were scattered on Lake Geneva in Switzerland, an area Freddie loved. Others believe that a family member has them. In truth, their location is not publicly known.

As a tribute to their fallen partner, the surviving members re-released "Bohemian Rhapsody" with "These Are the Days of Our Lives." Profits from the sale of the single went to charity that helped people living with AIDS. A special sleeve was placed around the record. On it were these words:

> **❝AIDS Concerns Us All. The proceeds of this record will go to the Terrence Higgins Trust. Freddie Mercury was concerned about that financial support be available to those less fortunate than himself, and therefore the money raised by this record will go to the home care of people living with AIDS and to health education campaigns to help prevent the further spread of the virus.❞**

As could be expected, the single topped the charts in the United Kingdom. In December 1991, Queen could claim ten albums on the U.K. Top-100 charts. Queen fans were paying their own tribute to Freddie, too, and helping a worthy cause.

Freddie would have liked that, too.

It did not seem possible that the band could go on without Freddie. After all, if one thought about Queen, the image of Freddie bounding across the concert stage immediately popped into mind. Freddie was the lead singer, the showman, the face of Queen. Now that he was gone, what future could Queen have? Freddie was irreplaceable.

John, Brian, and Roger had something bigger on their minds. Freddie had been more than a band mate. He had been their friend, and they needed to find the perfect way to honor him and tell him good-bye.

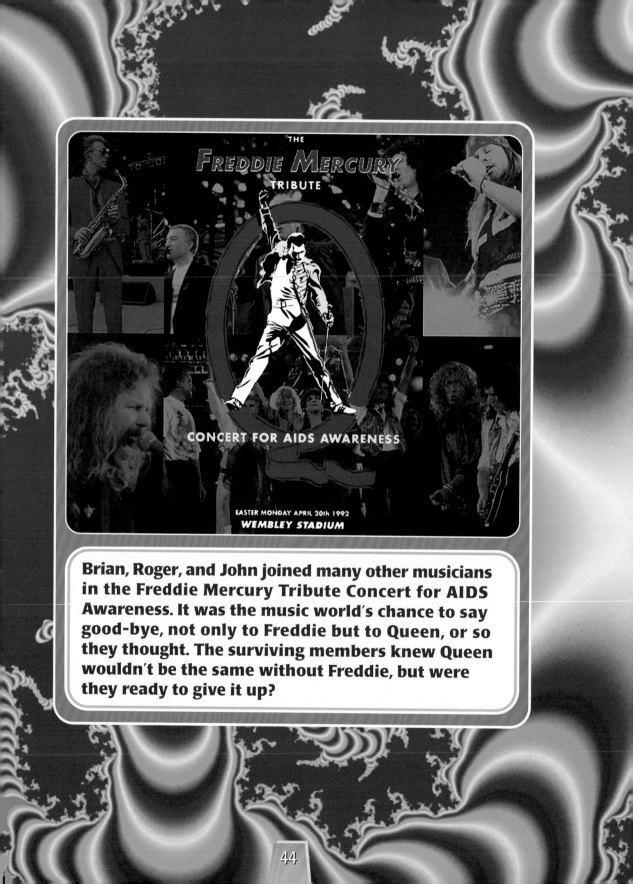

THE
FREDDIE MERCURY
TRIBUTE

CONCERT FOR AIDS AWARENESS

EASTER MONDAY APRIL 20th 1992
WEMBLEY STADIUM

Brian, Roger, and John joined many other musicians in the Freddie Mercury Tribute Concert for AIDS Awareness. It was the music world's chance to say good-bye, not only to Freddie but to Queen, or so they thought. The surviving members knew Queen wouldn't be the same without Freddie, but were they ready to give it up?

5

Long Live Queen

The best way to honor Freddie was obvious—through music. But it had to be something big, and it had to be the best. With that in mind, John, Roger, and Brian sought a way to honor their friend and to raise money for AIDS. Before long, the Freddie Mercury Tribute Concert began to take form.

John, Roger, and Brian formed the Mercury Phoenix Trust to handle the money side of their tribute projects and began to line up the stars to perform at the concert at Wembley Stadium on April 20, 1992. The concert was to be a happy occasion, a chance for fans and musicians to celebrate Freddie's life rather than mourn his passing.

There was no shortage of musicians who wanted to take part in the tribute concert. Robert Plant, Annie Lennox, Roger Daltrey, Def Leppard, Metallica, Elton John, David Bowie, and even Liza Minnelli were just a few of the artists who joined John, Roger, and Brian to perform Queen's biggest hits. Millions all over the world were able to watch the televised concert. The tribute raised a great deal of money for AIDS.

Still Queen?

Despite what many people think, John, Roger, and Brian never officially dissolved the group, though in some ways, Queen existed in name only. The last album with original material (other than greatest-hits type collections) was released in 1995. For *Made in Heaven*, John, Roger, and Brian combined material Freddie had worked on in 1991 with some not used on other albums. They even re-mastered tracks from Freddie's solo album. Brian and Roger have joined efforts to work on AIDS-related music projects. In 1997, John joined Brian and Roger to record "No-One But You (Only the Good Die Young)" for *Queen Rocks*, which was released that year. It was the last time the three performed together.

John retired in the late 1990s, but Roger and Brian weren't ready to say good-bye to Queen. They just weren't sure how to proceed.

Moving On

Brian and Roger continued to perform as Queen at charity events and award ceremonies, but they were generally billed as Queen +. Brian and Roger recorded and performed together, along with such "+"s as Wyclef Jean, George Michael, and Elton John.

In 1998, Brian released his first solo album since 1993. *Another World* refers to what Brian's life might have been like had he not discovered music. In college, he had studied astronomy. (Brian always maintained his interest in astronomy and science. In 2006, he published the book *Bang: The Complete History of the Universe*.) A portion of the proceeds of U.K. album sales were donated to the World Society for the Protection of Animals, a favorite charity of Cozy Powell, a drummer who appears on the album. Cozy was killed in a car accident, and Brian wanted to honor him.

Getting Its Props

For a band that was so incredibly popular, the group received few awards during its heyday. In the years since Freddie's death, however, the rock world has come to recognize Queen's influence. In 1999, the VH1 series *Legends* profiled Freddie, Brian, Roger, and John.

Brian released a solo album, *Another World*, in 1998. But his talents aren't limited to making music. In 2006, he cowrote a book, *Bang: The Complete History of the Universe*. Brian studied astronomy in school, and he had kept up his interest while a member of one of rock's hottest bands.

In September 1999, Queen was on the list of candidates for election into the Rock and Roll Hall of Fame. The group didn't get the required number of votes, and it would have to wait until 2000. In its second year of eligibility, Queen was voted into the hall as a member of the Class of 2001. Also elected that year was Freddie's friend, Michael Jackson.

After the induction ceremonies, members of the press asked Dave Grohl if he had felt any pressure singing the songs made so famous by Freddie Mercury since the late frontman's mother was in the audience:

"For the last maybe four or five nights, I've been listening to the live version and the studio version and the live version and the studio version, and just knowing that his mother was out in the audience, she was the only one I felt any responsibility for."

Rumors, Controversy, and More Honors

The year 2000 also brought rumors of a tour and recording sessions. Robbie Williams was one of the hottest acts in the United Kingdom. After word leaked out that Brian and Roger had been jamming with Robbie, rumors began to swirl that they would be touring together.

Though a tour didn't materialize, Queen and Robbie did work together in 2001. The three recorded a new version of the Queen megahit "We Are the Champions" for the film *A Knight's Tale* starring Heath Ledger. Robbie sang the lead, originally done by Freddie.

A strange kind of award also came Queen's way in 2001. Almost everyone can play air guitar, and some air guitarists take their song selection quite seriously. In 2001, Queen's "Bohemian Rhapsody" was voted by survey respondents as the #1 greatest air guitar song of all time. It might be a strange kind of award to receive, but again, it shows appreciation for a group who gave so much to their fans.

Queen Hits the Stage

Freddie often said that he was always looking for other ways to use Queen's music. He would be thrilled with the latest venue for Queen's songs—the theater. After six years of working on the

The Dominion Theatre in London was home to *We Will Rock You*, a musical featuring the music of Queen. Standing on the marquee of the Dominion is a statue of Freddie, surveying Queen's adoring fans as they enter the theater. The musical was a smash hit and has been staged in the United States, Canada, and Australia, among other venues.

project, *We Will Rock You* opened at the famous Dominion Theatre on London's West End on May 14, 2002.

Ben Elton wrote the musical. Brian and Roger also helped in creating it, as did the legendary American actor Robert DeNiro. On the Web site http://music.yahoo.com/read/news/12049995, Brian tells why it took so long to get the production off the ground:

"There's been many different script ideas. . . . The beginning was that we looked at the autobiographical approach and pursued it for a long time, and it just became something that didn't work for us. . . . And then Ben came up with this unbelievable idea for things which happen in the future, and we just thought, 'This is the perfect vehicle.'"

When the Queen musical *We Will Rock You* was staged in Germany, cast members took the show outside the walls of the theater. When Munich's new soccer stadium opened in May 2005, the musical's performers put on a rousing show for the audience, perhaps introducing many in the audience to a new experience.

In the future portrayed by *We Will Rock You*, computers are responsible for creating music. Human freedom and individual expression are things of the past. According to the play's author, his inspiration was "*The Matrix* meets the Arthurian legend meets *Terminator 2*."

Featured in the play are twenty-five of the group's biggest hits, including "Bohemian Rhapsody," "Another One Bites the Dust," "We Are the Champions," and "Crazy Little Thing Called Love." And because it is about Queen, it had to be showy. The production includes laser light effects and huge television screens—plasma of course.

The musical proved that there was still an audience for Queen's music. Audiences were made up of people who were fans of the group when it was big, as well as those who believed they were witnessing the cutting-edge of a new sound. Parents brought their children, and both age groups enjoyed the show. *We Will Rock You* was scheduled to close in London in October 2006, but public demand caused the theater to extend the run of the show indefinitely. The play has been staged in Barcelona, Spain; Sydney, Australia; Cologne, Germany; Kuala Lumpur, Malaysia; and Las Vegas, Nevada, as well as many other locations, all to overwhelmingly enthusiastic crowds.

Queen and the Queen

In 2002, Queen met the Queen. At a party to celebrate Queen Elizabeth II's Jubilee, a celebration of her fifty years on the British throne, some of the country's most famous rock stars had the chance to perform before Her Majesty, as well as a worldwide television audience of an estimated 200 million. Besides Queen, others on the bill included Paul McCartney, Ozzy Osbourne, Eric Clapton, Phil Collins, Rod Stewart, and Joe Cocker.

Anyone who thought that because these rockers were "older," they didn't have "it" anymore quickly learned otherwise. Brian started the party with the traditional "God Save the Queen." Well, as traditional as a member of Queen can make it. He played the normally reserved song on his guitar, loudly, while standing on the roof of the palace. According to an article in the June 6, 2002, issue of *The Daily Mail*, a London newspaper, "Queen's music was clearly one of the great features of the event." The group also performed "Bohemian Rhapsody" to thunderous cheers and applause from the crowd.

As of 2002, fans could walk all over Queen, the band, when it became a part of sidewalk history. Queen received a star on Hollywood's Walk of Fame.

Queen again found itself on top of a best-of chart as the year came to a close. Almost 190,000 people voted "Bohemian Rhapsody" the #1 single ever released in the United Kingdom. "Innuendo" and "Under Pressure," the group's duet with David Bowie, also made the list. Freddie's solo "Living on My Own" made the list at #86.

Queen + Paul Rodgers

The year 2002 had proved to Brian and Roger, as well as to some music writers and critics, that Queen could still draw a crowd. Its work was earning honors as well. In 2003, Queen became the first group to be inducted into the Songwriters Hall of Fame. Queen is the only group in which all lead members have written a #1 hit. In 2003, as Queen + Nelson Mandela, featuring Treana Morris, they recorded four songs for Nelson Mandela's 46664 campaign against AIDS.

The following year, "Bohemian Rhapsody" was voted into the Grammy Hall of Fame, though the group had never won a Grammy. In 2004, Queen was inducted into the Rock Walk of Fame. These **accolades** for the group's past work were welcome and appreciated, but Brian and Roger weren't content to rest on what had once been. They wanted to perform and record again.

In 2004, Roger and Brian were at the U.K. Music Hall of Fame Awards and wanted to play live for the televised show. Brian asked Paul Rodgers, formerly with Free, Bad Company, and the Firm, if he would join Roger and him for the performance. Paul was flattered and agreed. The performance went so well and they had so much fun, that the guys wanted to do more. After some thought, Roger and Brian announced that Queen would re-form and begin touring in 2005. Paul would do the lead vocals, but Roger and Brian wanted to make sure everyone knew he wasn't replacing Freddie. There was only one Freddie. Paul was the featured singer, not technically a part of Queen. The group would be known as Queen + Paul Rodgers.

Replacing the retired John Deacon on bass was Danny Miranda of the Blue Öyster Cult. Also joining the group were Spike Edney and Jamie Moses, both of whom had worked with Brian and Roger before.

Even many years after Freddie's death, Queen still supports AIDS causes. In 2003, they participated in Nelson Mandela's 46664 campaign against AIDS in Africa. They returned to South Africa in 2005 to perform in another 46664 concert. But before the show, Paul Rodgers, Roger Taylor, and Brian May took time to meet children at the George Child and Welfare Society.

There will never be another Freddie Mercury, and Brian and Roger want the fans to know that. So, when Paul Rodgers came onboard to sing vocals, the group's name was changed to Queen + Paul Rodgers. The band is touring extensively, introducing a new generation to the music of Queen.

Queen + Paul Rodgers have played to enthusiastic audiences in the United Kingdom, the United States, and Japan, among others. In late 2006, the group announced that they were getting together to do an album, which would be released in 2007.

Queen Hits the Big Time—*American Idol*

In 2006, the music of Queen was featured on the hit U.S. television show *American Idol*. The guys worked with the contestants, who were required to sing Queen songs during the week's competition. Contestant Ace Young wanted to sing Brian's "We Will Rock You" R&B style. Television audiences saw Brian argue with Ace, but according to Brian, editing cut out most of the discussion, and in truth, he didn't have a big problem with Ace.

That wasn't the first time Queen was associated with the program, though it was the only time they were *directly* involved with it. In 2004, *American Idol*'s most famous loser—William Hung—released a cover of "We Are the Champions." William's vocal talent is limited, but he's made good money out of being bad. When he was asked for his thoughts about William's rendition, Brian stated that he had no problem with William's version of the song.

Queen's past performances still bring them honors. In a poll of musicians and music critics in 2005, Queen's performance at 1985's Live Aid was voted the greatest live show of all time. VH1 included Queen among its first group of metal honorees in 2006. Also in 2006, Queen's *Greatest Hits* was named the best-selling album of all time in the United Kingdom, winning over the Rolling Stones and the Beatles among others. And in 2007, Queen was voted the Best British Band of All Time.

It appears as though 2007 will also bring a long-awaited album from Queen + Paul Rodgers and more concerts. Without Freddie it won't be the same, but Queen fans are still excited.

1971 **June** Queen plays its first public concert.

1973 Queen releases its first album, *Queen.*

1974 Queen tours Australia, which is disastrous.

Sheer Heart Attack brings Queen its first international success.

1975 *A Night at the Opera*, featuring "Bohemian Rhapsody," is released.

Queen tours the United States for the first time.

Queen tours Japan.

1976 Queen returns to the United States for a tour; sales and airplay of "Bohemian Rhapsody" and *A Night at the Opera* soar as a result.

Queen makes a triumphant tour of Australia.

September Queen performs at a free concert in Hyde Park, London.

1980 *The Game* is released and becomes the group's highest-selling, non–greatest-hits album of all time.

At the urging of Michael Jackson, "Another One Bites the Dust" is released as a single; it becomes the first song to place on the *Billboard* Rock, R&B, and Dance charts at the same time.

1981 **February** "Crazy Little Thing Called Love" becomes Queen's first #1 single in the United States.

Queen becomes the first major rock band to play concerts in South America and Mexico, setting attendance records along the way.

Queen collaborates with David Bowie on the song "Under Pressure."

1982 Queen tours the United States for the last time.

1984 **September 15** Queen performs a series of concerts in South Africa.

1985 Queen breaks attendance record when it performs at the Rock in Rio festival.

Queen gives a phenomenal performance at Live Aid.

1986 **August 9** Queen performs at Knebworth Stadium, its 685th, and last, concert.

1991 **November 24** Freddie Mercury dies.

1992 **April 20** The surviving members of Queen coordinate a concert at Wembley Stadium to celebrate Freddie's life.

1995 The group's last album of original material (other than greatest-hits collections) is released.

1997 John, Roger, and Brian perform together for the last time.

2001 **March 19** Queen is inducted into the Rock and Roll Hall of Fame.

In a poll, "Bohemian Rhapsody" is voted the greatest air guitar song of all time.

2002 Queen plays at the Queen's Jubilee party.

Queen receives a star on Hollywood's Walk of Fame.

We Will Rock You, a musical based on Queen's music, opens at the Dominion Theatre in London.

Almost 190,000 people voted "Bohemian Rhapsody" the #1 single ever released in the United Kingdom.

2003 Queen becomes the first group inducted into the Songwriters Hall of Fame.

2004 Queen is inducted into the United Kingdom Music Hall of Fame.

"Bohemian Rhapsody" is voted into the Grammy Hall of Fame.

Queen is inducted into the Rock Walk of Fame.

2005 Paul Rodgers teams with Queen to perform as Queen + Paul Rodgers.

In a poll of critics and musicians, Queen's performance at Live Aid is chosen the greatest live show of all time.

2006 Queen is featured on *American Idol*.

Queen's *Greatest Hits* is named the best-selling album of all time in the United Kingdom.

Queen is honored at the VH1 Rock Honors.

2007 Queen is voted the Best British Band of All Time in a U.K. poll.

Albums

1973   *Queen I*

1974   *Queen II*
       Sheer Heart Attack

1975   *A Night at the Opera*

1976   *A Day at the Races*

1977   *News of the World*

1978   *Jazz*

1979   *Live Killers*

1980   *The Game*

1981   *Flash Gordon*
       Greatest Hits

1982   *Hot Space*

1984   *The Works*

1986   *A Kind of Magic*

1989   *The Miracle*

1991   *Innuendo*

1992   *Classic Queen*
       Live at the Wembley
       Greatest Hits

1995   *Greatest Hits I & II*
       Queen at the BBC
       Made in Heaven

1996   *Live Magic*

1997   *Queen Rocks*

1999   *Greatest Hits III*

2005   *A Night at the Opera*

Number-One Singles

1979   "Crazy Little Thing Called Love"

1980   "Another One Bites the Dust"

Videos

1986 *Queen—Live at Wembley '86*

1991 *Rocumentary*

1999 *Princes of the Universe*

2002 *The Freddie Mercury Tribute Concert*
Queen—Greatest Video Hits I

2003 *Queen—Greatest Video Hits II*
2004 *Queen—Magic Moments*
Queen—On Fire at the Bowl

2006 *On the Rock Trail—Queen*
Queen—Under Review: 1980–91

Selected Television Appearances

1977 *The Midnight Special*

1982 *Saturday Night Live*

1998 *Parkinson*

2006 *American Idol*

Awards

1975 *Sound* Readers' Poll Awards: Best Band, Best Album (*A Night at the Opera*), Best Single ("Bohemian Rhapsody").

1977 Brit Award: Best Single of the Last 25 Years ("Bohemian Rhapsody").

1990 Brit Award: Outstanding Contributions to British Music.

1992 Brit Award: Best Single ("These Are the Days of Our Lives").

2001 Inducted into Rock and Roll Hall of Fame.

2002 Receives star on the Hollywood Walk of Fame.

2003 Inducted into the Rock and Roll Hall of Fame.

2004 Grammy Award: "Bohemian Rhapsody" is inducted into the Grammy Hall of Fame.

Queen inducted into the United Kingdom Music Hall of Fame and Rock Walk Hall of Fame.

2006 Inducted into the VH1 Rock Honors.

Books

Freestone, Peter. *Freddie Mercury*. London: Omnibus Press, 2001

Freestone, Peter, and David West. *Freddie Mercury: An Intimate Memoir by the Man Who Knew Him Best*. London: Omnibus Press, 2000.

Hodkinson, Mark. *Queen: The Early Years*. London: Omnibus Press, 2004.

Purvis, Georg. *Queen: Complete Works*. Surrey, U.K.: Reynolds & Hearn, 2007.

Tedman, Ray. *Queen*. Surrey, U.K.: Reynolds & Hearn, 2005.

Web Sites

www.brianmay.com
Brian May

www.drummerworld.com/drummers/Roger_Taylor.html
Roger Taylor

ww.queenonline.com
Queen Online

www.queenonline.com/wewillrockyou/index_reg.html
We Will Rock You

www.queenpluspaulrodgers.com
Queen + Paul Rodgers

www.queenworld.com
Official International Queen Fan Club

wwww.queenzone.com
Queen Zone

www.rockhall.com
Rock and Roll Hall of Fame

a cappella—Sung without instrumental accompaniment.

accolades—Expressions of high praise.

blues—A style of music that developed from African American folk songs in the early twentieth century, consisting mainly of sad songs.

conjecture—Guesswork.

criteria—Accepted standards used in making decisions or judgments about something.

dissension—Disagreement.

funk—A musical style derived from jazz, blues, and soul and is characterized by a heavy rhythmic bass and backbeat.

genre—A category of artistic work.

gold—A designation that a recording has sold at least 500,000 copies.

gospel—Highly emotional music that originated among African American Christians in the southern United States.

inducted—Formally admitted into something, such as an organization.

medley—A continuous piece of music consisting of two or more different tunes or songs played one after the other.

platinum—A designation that a single has sold 1 million copies, or that an album or CD has sold 2 million copies.

pyrotechnics—Fireworks.

rockabilly—A style of pop music that originated in the late 1950s and combines elements of rock music with country music.

venues—Performance locations.

Peter Gregory had piano, violin, flute, and voice lessons as a child and teenager. As an adult, he plays the iPod and CD player. He is a freelance author living in New York.

Picture Credits

page

2: EMI/Parlophone/Star Photos

8: Jeff Kravit/FilmMagic

11: Stan Honda/AFP

12: Tsuni/iPhoto

14: EMI/Parlophone/Star Photos

17: BBC/Hulton Picture Library

18: EMI/Parlophone/Star Photos

21: Pictorial Press

23: Rare Pics Library

24: Mirrorpix

26: KRT/NMI

29: Mirrorpix

30: Pictorial Press

33: Mirrorpix

34: UPI Photo Archive

36: EMI/Parlophone/Star Photos

39: Rex Features

41: New Millennium Images

44: New Millennium Images

47: KRT/PRNPS

49: New Millennium Images

50: A3483/Deutsch Presse Agentur

53: Rajesh JantilalL/AFP/Getty Images

54: Sipa Press

Front cover: EMI/Parlophone/Star Photos